BAPTISM

by

Martin E. Marty

FORTRESS PRESS   ●   PHILADELPHIA

First paperback edition 1977
Fourth printing 1984

Library of Congress Cataloging in Publication Data
Marty, Martin E   1928-
  Baptism.
  1. Baptism. I. Title.
BV811.2.M3 1977   234′.161   77-78635
ISBN 0-8006-1317-1

1090B84   Printed in the United States of America   1–1317

Contents

Introduction

It is dark.

A shivering band of people has commandeered a cistern. In the depths of the earth the sound of moving water is heard. The slightest shuffling of feet echoes throughout the chamber. Most of the band are quiet, though a few whisper. Above the ground, heard only faintly from below, a rooster crows, marking the day's beginning. Soon farmers and merchants will be rising from sleep to take up their daily occupations, unaware of the activity underground. They would not understand the quiet rites, nor approve, and might even take action against the participants if they had knowledge and opportunity.

Meanwhile, below, a leader has come to the fore, a man of serene but slightly severe appearance. He whispers some words in the almost eerie setting. Some of the people begin to take off their clothes, folding them and setting them aside. With great solemnity and in many cases no little fear they approach the bowl of the cistern where water bubbles and flows. The children are put forward and dipped in first, after some questions which in many cases are answered for them. Then come the older children and the men. They are asked a number of very serious questions; after answering, and being placed under the water, they come out struck dumb by an experience of both physical and spiritual shock. Finally the women remove all their ornaments and loosen their hair. They are to have no alien objects, no rings or jewelry or band-

4

ages on them. Warily they step into the water and come out, dressing again in the now brightening glow of candles and torches.

The leader is very busy with various kinds of oil which he seems to be blessing and pouring on the people. He is asking questions and hearing answers and repeating formulas. Somehow his magisterial appearance and manner assuage the fright of the people near him. He seems satisfied with the proceedings, and gives orders for an exit to be prepared. The group makes its way through some passageways into a larger room. Here others who have themselves undergone the experience on an earlier occasion greet them warmly and invite them to a meal of bread and wine at which sacred words are spoken and hymns are sung. The people now seem relieved and are obviously happy.

They have been baptized.

The event—with all the hazards of the mystic and the overdramatic—has been described more or less after the manner of the *traditio apostolica,* the apostolic tradition of Hippolytus in the earliest Christian centuries.

It is light.

A group of people are gathered off to the side in front of a large room full of onlookers. The sun is streaming in, its light broken into colorful fragments as it passes through a window. This window is different from most; it is made of stained glass, and under it is a very large bronze plaque which says: "To remember the good works of Mary Taylor, placed here by her husband." A man wearing long black and white and green clothes—for this time and place a strange combination as all the other people are wearing street clothes—beckons the smaller gathering of people over to a sort of finger bowl on a marble stand.

They move toward it, somewhat ill at ease, but generally undisturbed by the whole procedure. Outside, the motor of a power mower starts to roar, for it is 11:15 in the morning and American suburbanites are beginning to awaken to their sacred outdoor Sunday rites. The accumulation of cars in the parking lot and the sound of song coming through the open windows suggest that something is going on inside the big building. But the gardeners and grass cutters are neither disturbed by the noise nor curious about the ceremonies. They do not even turn their heads to look in, though some heads inside are turned to look out. The soothing ripple of sound emanates from an electronic organ which provides quiet background music for the ceremony—silence is abhorred by the gathered people. The man with the long clothes on begins to read.

One of the people up front is carrying a baby, a healthy-looking half-year-old who through careful overfeeding has been induced into somnolence—nothing he does should be allowed to disturb the decor and manners of this impressive setting. The child wears a blue suit with pink lambs embroidered on it. His hair is combed to perfection, and his mother is hoping that the man will not have to mess it up too much. Passingly she wonders whether she turned off the oven or whether her dinner for all the guests will be ruined. Father too is watching the proceedings, with an envelope in his pocket which he will give the minister as payment for his trouble. He is happy with himself: he was able to arrange a Sunday on the church schedule when both sets of the baby's grandparents could be here, and to lay in a supply of the best vintage champagne for a christening breakfast. He hopes to get out of the building afterwhile without becoming too involved in conversation with the man in long clothes who will move to the door before the rest of the people.

The "godparents," meanwhile, are smiling down at the baby; he seems so *cute* lying there smiling while the man describes a cross on his forehead and breast. They were glad they talked the parents into "having it done." It's better to be on the safe side, they figured; anyway all children really ought to be christened. The man dips his finger into the little bowl three times and says some words: they hear a prayer. The godmother turns and walks down the aisle, conscious of how the child's light blue matches her own new dress. The other people in the room smile, pleased at how things have gone: the baby was just precious and the whole thing provided a bit of variety from the usual routine.

The child will probably be back in four years. His parents will want to drop him at the door of the Sunday School for supervised play activities. When he reaches the eighth grade he may even be sent back to prepare for simultaneous graduation from church. The cycles of the generations will move on—before too many years he may even be having all this done for his child too.

He has been baptized.

The event—with all the hazards of the nonmysterious and the underdramatic—has been described more or less after the manner of the *traditio protestantica,* the Protestant tradition in the twentieth Christian century.

The Christian believes that *God* can work the same benefits in both these baptisms.

The Christian asks whether *man* can take the same benefits from both.

This question, which exercises so many thoughtful people in the church today, is the main theme of this brief study of the water of life. The book will concentrate on baptism as practiced by those evangelical catholic Christians (people who are both gospel oriented and have their eye on historic and universal Christian belief and practice) who baptize both infants and adults. It may be read by adults preparing for baptism, by parents or godparents bringing their charges to baptism, and by people interested in recent thought about baptism. Most of all, it is designed for reflective Christian people who would like to make more use of the benefits God has given with this water of life, and actually endeavor to *live* their baptism.

These will ordinarily be people who regularly hear the Word of God and regularly celebrate the presence of Christ in the Lord's Supper. They may regard themselves as handicapped in their understanding of baptism because it is something that happens only once—and in their case, happening as it did long before they were even conscious of it, hence belongs to the past. Some of them at least will be surprised to learn that baptism does not only happen once and that it belongs to the present. It happens every morning, in every act of repentance, and in every response to the loving gift of God in Christ. It could even be happening now as the Spirit may make himself heard through these pages.

What Is Baptism?

People who have even the slightest awareness of the meaning of baptism, one of the two sacraments regularly observed in most Protestant churches, will have no problem with this first point. It is quite obvious that baptism is not simply water, because it takes place in conscious connection with certain questions, words, and formulas, and is enacted in specific settings and with the use of particular ceremonies. Ordinarily the gathered group of Christians surrounds the act as they would not surround any other use of water in connection with a child.

Apart from that, however, Christians are coming to learn again that there is nothing that is "simply water." Great thinkers and teachers of the church are working to help them understand that water, with all creation, is dependent on the Word of a creating God. In a scientific, technical, and coldly surgical world men of the modern city are being called again to faith in God as Creator. They are recovering an understanding of the common elements of life, the earth, air, fire, and water. Most of all, after generations of seeing much in Christianity reduced to flattened-out reasonableness and humanly-generated piety, they are learning again that God works through visible means: bread and wine, lips, hands, and this element of water.

So water is never "simply water" for the simple reason that it is called out of nothingness into being by the Word of God; it is lifted out of nullity into effectiveness by the saving Word, and is part of God's plan to introduce new holiness into the world. In the modern city man has forgotten much of the natural properties of the water which God through his Word introduces into his new creation. In the back of his mind modern man may be aware of the fact that most of the earth's surface is water. He can remove himself from the world of factories and commuter trains to the world of nature he has left behind. There is mist, dew, droplet, rain, torrent; rivulet, brook, creek, river, whirlpool; there is lake and most of all the boundless depths of the sea. There is water which keeps his lawn alive and his children clean and his body nourished. He knows that water produces power, cleanliness, life; it can be evaporated, frozen, changed. Because it is upheld by the Word of the Lord who made the heavens it is never "simply water."

He will not quibble about words, however. For mere water is not regarded anyway as carrying all the possibilities which baptismal water is said to bear. In the matter of conveying grace and bringing man into the family of God it is indeed nothing. In the matter of seeing man justified by God water would be "simply water" were it not for the special situation in which it is placed. Because this emphasis on the water is part of our age's recovery of the Bible's fullness, however, we do well to linger longer, to be reminded that while baptism is not simply water, yet—

. . . IT IS THE WATER . . .

and its elemental character is to be reflected upon. God is the Creator, and he cares for his creation. He does not leave it to its own devices simply because man in his sin misuses it. The creation is never abandoned by God, even though Christian people would sometimes abandon it. Protestants often complain about the "worldliness," the secularism and materialism of people who care only for the natural processes of the age, for what they can see, handle, and own. But it is this very disregard on the part of Christians for the "water" and what it symbolizes that has contributed to the situation they deplore. Someone has compared this complaining about naturalism and worldliness to the bewailing of two fair-haired parents who reproach a fair-haired child for not being dark.

This failure on the part of Christians to understand creation, its elements, its devices—its "water"—did not come about only because of bad men in the church but because of good men who, being compelled in their situation to emphasize one aspect of an argument, had to let go for the moment of other realities. Their sons and daughters, picking up the pieces of this legacy in a different time and place, have to re-explore its neglected portions. I am referring now to the authors of the Reformation catechisms and to their books of instruction, through which generations of children have since been taught the meaning of baptism, books whose hidden depths have yet to be fully explored.

These writings of the sixteenth century are little concerned with the doctrine of creation in relation to baptism and its water. Their authors were fighting then a battle just the opposite of that which the church is fighting today in an urban, unbelieving world. They stressed in their time the power of the Word with which God in Christ instituted the sacraments. They emphasized the "mereness" of water because they were engaged in reforming a church that had over-believed, over-regarded the inherent, mysterious, magical, superstitious qualities of water. In their day, because of baptism, holy water was commonly being used to cure everything, to bless everything; it was splashed around indiscriminately, and powers verging on the idolatrous were ascribed to it. Water was used as a bond between man's aspiration and God. It was part of a merit badge system; one could, as it were, swim or cleanse his own way into heaven. Along the way faith in the Word of God was often neglected.

Someone has observed that if the Reformers could see the cheapness with which grace is asserted today, the ethical disinterest, the nonchalant drift of people into the family of God, they would assert virtually the opposite of what they did in their own time. Then they were faced by a legal system which often had a tyrannous and horrific side. They shouted "man is justified by faith." But their shout is meaningless in the ears of a modern who considers himself saved because he possesses the modern conveniences and shares the inherent respectability of Our Way of Life. So with baptism: fighting superstition and the merit-seeking impulse the Reformers understandably minimized the fact that what Christ actually commanded was baptism with water, that real water was involved. Today, fighting unbelief, secularism, and heedlessness, many of their sons are asking again about the purpose of God in instituting visible means of conveying his Word.

This is particularly important in the Reformation churches, where the *whole* Bible, not just one of its Testaments or accents, is regarded. It is true, of course, that one accent must be seen to interpret all the others. The Reformers were right, timelessly right, in thus interpreting the plan of God. They told us what will be asserted in every page of this book, that the only joy the Christian should seek is the joy of the forgiveness of sins. He should taste and see that the Lord is sweet by savoring the character of God in the benefits of Jesus Christ. He should not for the moment be diverted from this activity by concern with magic or merit. But it is this very joy of forgiveness which sends the believer back out into the world of water and sun, of light and cereal, of engines and ballots and washing machines. Baptism intends the totality of the forgiven life in the midst of the world. Despite their de-emphasis of it the Reformers did not do away with the water in baptism. Our task is to uncover certain aspects of the view of the world which our fathers could assume but which come so hard today.

So the Christian who is baptized clings only to the Word of forgiveness. But he finds that Word set in a revelation to which the whole Bible witnesses; and a host of pictures, symbols, signs, events, and realities come to his mind if he has been informed about the plan of God. He begins to inquire about the origin of baptism. He may know that many religions have ceremonial washings, and that most of them, like Christianity, use them pre-eminently as initiation or entrance rites. The Christian faith claims no uniqueness for its ceremonies as regards their natural side. It is not afraid to explore the many parallels to its acts in other religions and in the mental make-up of men. Its uniqueness lies in its witness to what God, the Father of Jesus Christ, can make of such ceremonial acts. The Christian may know that in Judaism water had a number of sacred uses and that, here and there, there are even slight hints which prefigure some aspects of Christian baptism. These hints belong to the era of promise, however; they do not in any way negate the originality of the gift of God in Christ. Anyone who has made a study of Christian history may have become conscious of the growing practice of ceremonial washings in the later Judaism of the time of Christ. The recently discovered Dead Sea scrolls, and the newly excavated monasteries of some ancient Essene sects have heightened our interest in the natural roots of baptism.

The rise of "proselyte baptism," an introductory ceremony through which pagans who became Jews by profession were received, cannot be dated with accuracy.

But we do know that by the time John the Baptist began his work along the lower banks of the Jordan his reason for using water could have been easily understood by the people—though to be sure the basic newness of his use of it was also apparent. Crowds gathered. He preached that men should be wrenched from their past. They should renounce their claims on God. They should empty their hands and their ears and their hearts. They should be willing to be turned around completely (*metanoia*) in repentance. Newness was breaking in. The kingdom of God was at hand.

John's work belonged to a pivotal period of history. The decisively new began one day when a young man of Nazareth named Jesus was attracted to the banks of the Jordan. He too stepped into the water. John had been preaching that his own baptism was for the forgiving of sins after repentance. Here was one who, he was given to see, was the Righteous One of God, who had no sin, no need for repentance, no possibility of being forgiven. To baptize him on the usual terms would have been at best meaningless and at worst a negation, a blasphemy. Yet the man from Nazareth said that this baptism must occur. It was "to fulfill all righteousness." In that act Jesus identified himself with the plan of God's righteousness. He was himself the suffering servant of whom the second Isaiah had spoken. He was the anointed of God. From now on he could speak of his purposes as a "baptism" of suffering. On Golgotha "a general baptism of all men" would occur, which would give rise to the particular baptism of all the people of God. To fulfill all righteousness Jesus identified himself with his people, he participated in the commonness of their life.

He stepped into the water and was baptized.

A voice made clear that in this identification, this humility or weakness, the strength of God was revealed among men: "This is my beloved Son." A dove such as had brooded over the Flood waters, the Spirit who had brooded over the primeval waters of Genesis was seen to confirm and seal the act.

Jesus was baptized. In his resurrected life, claiming all authority—as the words at the end of the Gospel of Matthew tell us—he was heard to send out his disciples to make disciples of all nations, baptizing them in the name of the Father, and of the Son, and of the Holy Ghost. This became the verbal formula at baptisms before long, though the very first baptisms recorded in the Book of Acts usually accented the name of Jesus.

So the church, from the first, baptized. It used this water of life in homes, and also in the synagogues until the Christian movement was displaced. Baptisms were performed in streets and rivers and jails, and later in church buildings, in cisterns and catacombs. The church did not baptize with honey or milk or the drippings of pomegranate. It used water, after the ordinance of God. The Book of Acts describes the outreach of the church in a dazzling pattern of concentrics: from Jerusalem to the parts of Judea to Galilee to Samaria to the uttermost parts of the earth. At each decisive turn baptism was the first step: for the thousands at Pentecost after a wonderful sign had been worked; by Philip in Samaria; for the Ethiopian eunuch; for Saul-turned-Paul, the greatest missioner the church has known. Then it became a contagion as of fire: in Antioch, and for Lydia and the jailer as Paul moved into Europe from Asia. Throughout Christian history it has always been a first step: the baptism of Clovis, the baptisms in the northlands, the baptisms by Francis Xavier who claimed to have baptized 900,000 people "in the uttermost parts of the earth." And always, with water.

Christian baptism of adults has ordinarily been associated with intensive instruction. There have been exceptions of course. In the earliest period of urgent grace, men newly faced with the claim of God in Christ would ask, "What is to prevent my being baptized?" And, if water was present, they were baptized. In the latest period of cheap grace, men casually faced with the name of God in Christ could shake a minister's hand, pledge themselves to a fellowship, and be baptized with a minimum of instruction. Apart from such exceptions, however, where instruction has been intensive and where preachers have regarded the values of baptism in their spoken word, there has been considerable exploration of the biblical uses of water.

The Christian life is a recapitulation, a summary in the life of the church of much of the activity of God, who in Christ identified himself with man "to fulfill all righteousness." His life was a recapitulation, a summary, a microcosm, a miniature of the plan of God for his ancient people. So it is that in Christ the births, deliverances, and cleansings by water throughout the whole Bible are called to mind. In the ancient Near East water had been the home of the monsters of the abyss, the dragons of the depths; it was the home of death from which God's man would have to be snatched. Water existed as the chief form of the primeval chaos and confusion. It was called out of nothingness into something by the Word of God. It was called out of disorder into order; it was given boundary and was parted by the activity of God. The Spirit of God brooded and hovered over the depths.

When man sinned and the world was inundated, God delivered his own in the midst of the Flood. When he led his people from bondage they were brought through the Red Sea in a passage from death to life. When Job questioned God, he was given clear instructions on his own place by being related to the mysterious depths and power of the waters. The Psalmist mused over the profundities of water. John and Jesus made the trip to the Jordan. Before he was crucified Jesus first washed the disciples' feet. He who was and is the water of life, the living water, experienced a gushing of blood and water from his side in death. Just as the whole language of Calvary presupposes the Old Testament sacrifice of a lamb with blood, so the whole language of baptism presupposes a biblical interest in water.

The Christian says: Baptism is my departure out of chaos into the order of the forgiven life. It is my visitation by the Spirit which broods over this water of life. It is my deliverance from the destroying floods, my passage through the Red Seas of sin and enmity. I am humbled by it as was Job, inspired by it as was the Psalmist. Baptism is my trip to the Jordan. In this water I am crucified with Christ; nevertheless I live, sharing his living water. None of these events, activities, pictures, signs, symbols, pre- or post-figurations distract from the one meaning, that here I seek and find the joy of forgiveness. Rather they are the countless colors that add riches to the full portrait. They are the grace notes that parallel God's melodic line. They are the story of my life, a life which is born in baptism. They all deal with water and with the Word of the One who restores me to life. They are my waters of Siloam and my pool of Bethesda, my entrance to the new life of the kingdom: thoughts such as these could well occupy any Christian who observes someone else's baptism.

To the Christian, then, water is not a mere nothing. Called into being by God and consecrated by his Spirit it is made into a something, a gracious water of life, by a new, clear, particular Word. Something happens to it. It is not simply water, but it *is* water.

This understanding has practical consequences. It should inform Christian preaching and meditation on creation and rebirth or forgiveness. In subtle ways (we do not delude ourselves that major reforms in this area are possible) it may even shape the act of baptism itself. There is no doubt that the early church ordinarily immersed people entirely or at least used a great deal of water. For reasons that will be clear later, numbers of the Reformers who did not practice immersion at least regretted its disuse and wished for its return. Nevertheless the trend through the centuries has been away from the early understanding which involved relishing, drowning in, and enjoying the water of life. The baptismal river became a pool; the pool became a well or cistern; the cistern became a barrel; the barrel became a font; the font became a birdbath; the birdbath became a bowl; the bowl became a finger bowl. If the trend continues—perhaps it is not irreverent to ask—shall we soon be experiencing the waters, the Flood, the Red Sea, the Jordan, the water of life in the minuscule antisepsis of an aerator, an atomizer, or a humidifier?

Since tradition, architecture, and the shape of bowls are slow to change, ministers and other baptizers could at least indicate by their handling of it that water is the very element God has chosen to visit and use with his grace. It might be a good practice to use the element less sparingly. God can of course work through any water in any amount, if so he promises. But the man who tastes to see that the Lord is sweet should really be permitted to taste. Man is, in baptism, not what man was by nature, but what he experiences. And the people who witness the experience of this water in the hearing and faith in the Word of God should at least be permitted to suffer through and then delight in the experience. Thus one more element of the biblical understanding can come through.

The joy in the creation experienced by the person who

has known the joy of forgiveness comes only by the initiative and activity of God. For baptism is not simply water; it is the water—

... COMPREHENDED IN GOD'S COMMAND ...

Single-minded focusing on the origin of baptism in the plan of God serves to purge the mind of any magical conceptions concerning the sacrament. The churches of the Reformation resisted the idea technically known as the *ex opere operato* efficacy of baptism. That is, they rejected the common notion that merely by the act of going through a baptism everything that needed to be effected had been done. Their position was complicated by two factors. In the first place, with St. Augustine and the main strand of Christian history they affirmed that the faith of the baptizer did not play a part. Augustine had opposed those who argued long ago—after some Christians who had defected in the face of persecution later returned to the church and were suspected of hypocrisy —that the sacraments depended on the faith and character of their human enacters. The Reformers likewise said no. They were interested in pinning man's whole security on but one hook, the loving initiative of God, lest men should rely on other men and hence be haunted by the wrong kinds of insecurity.

Not only did the Reformers de-emphasize the faith of the baptizers; they also (with the exception of the "Anabaptists") in the second place retained the existing practice of baptizing infants. Since faith was usually defined as a response, a trusting or assenting or having confidence in, it was clear that these portions of the definition of faith did not apply in the case of a child not yet conscious of what is happening. The Reformers' double de-emphasis on the conventional activities of faith, however, almost seemed to make of baptism a mechanical, magical act. Indeed this view of the sacrament is at the heart of the modern Protestant notion that baptism is something we ought to "have done in order to be on the safe side" because everyone else has it done and because we do not know enough about what happens to those who neglect baptism to safely omit it.

There were many ways, however, in which the apparently mechanical was actually demechanized in Reformation teaching. Some of these we shall discuss later. But first and in many ways decisive was the careful understanding of what it means to carry out a command of God. This took the burden off the humanly-achieved-and -sustained faith of the baptizer on the one hand, and the magic of a child's response on the other, and placed it on the responding and obedient community of Jesus Christ. The believing community would follow God's command—even where they could not tie up all the meanings into intellectually neat patterns. They knew that nowhere did God call them into jibberish, tomfoolery, or nonsense. They knew that the surrender to which baptism and the faith called them was not a surrender of reason, logic, language, and sense. So far as they were concerned there was only one basic surprise, only one radical contradiction of their normal expectation, and that was the fact that God the eternal, the remote, the essential could actually visit and sustain the temporal, the near, the existing, and that he did just that in his Word, particularly in the Word made flesh in Jesus Christ. Once they were ready to receive this surprise, this gift, they could respond to the commands God gave them in and with it. And as they began to respond, they could work out the implications of their having received the gift. It is in this light that many of the steps the Reformers took to safeguard integrity and personal involvement in baptism begin to make sense. Here is where the bringing of children to God's house, and teaching and confirming them became an obligation of parent and church. Here, however, is also where various props for human frailty came to be devised to help hold up the center. Yet there can be only one center: not the magic of human action, not the merit of human faith, but the purpose of God in his command.

God's mandate to baptize has been recognized throughout the church in all its ages. Whether or not to baptize has seldom been the issue in the catholic Christian church. Occasionally there have been nonbaptizing sects. They existed in the early church and in the church of the Reformation, and still are found today. Even these, however, in trying to take seriously God's total command, have often developed surrogates for water baptism. Usually their heavy emphasis on the remoteness of God and on the spiritual character of man's response involved them in a denial of God's ability to use the material order to his purposes. But such interpretations have always belonged to the few; statistically and temporally they have been in the minority. In the ecumenical movement today the question whether God's command to baptize still demands response through the use of water and the Word is hardly an issue for discussion except among the Salvation Army and the Society of Friends or Quakers. For the vast bulk of Christians at all times and in all places debate has centered on such questions as the modes of baptism, the ages for baptism, and the meaning of baptism; but for all the "one baptism" is born out of the one command of God.

Since so many promises of God are connected with baptism it is fortunate that the early church and the canonical Scriptures preserve the words of command with such clarity. So much of the origin of baptism is lost

21

in mystery and history. Even the original setting of some of the baptismal commands—on which the Reformers of the church pinned so much—is often called into question. But the immediate and consistent practice of the church from earliest times indicates the presence of a command and the seriousness of the response. This is fortunate because the promises might well be lost if the Scriptures and the church did not so uniformly regard the gravity of the command. Suppose Jesus had said, "I recommend that you baptize people. It would be a nice little act which would be of help in the Christian life." Suppose an apostle had said, "I move that we act on this recommendation." It is not very likely that much of this would have been preserved. Indeed there were other practices which had little more than this to support them. Jesus said it would be exemplary to wash each other's feet. The general disinterest in foot washing as a symbol of humility and love shows what would have happened to baptism without the rigor of command: we would be deprived of its gift. James wrote that it would be salutary to have elders visit the sick with oil and prayers. The general disinterest in healing and oils as a symbol of God's concern for the body shows again what would have happened to baptism were this the only sanction.

Instead, as with the Lord's Supper, there is the command: "Do this!" "Go!" Like all demands of God, this call to repentance is absolutely serious, taut, tight, rigorous. Here is not merely a symbol of humility, an emblem of God's concern. Here is actually God himself acting in the midst of the believing community. While this command is accompanied—as in the case of all God's other mandates—by what Paul called the wrath of God, it exists primarily for the presence of God's holiness among men and for the good of men. So baptism is seen to be not the ordinance of any man but of the Man of God's own choosing. It is not just a nice little ceremony, a ritual that can be tampered with. An obedient and faithful church will seek to learn ever more about the origins, meaning, and intention of baptism both in its original setting and today, and then to act on what it learns.

One aspect of Christ's baptismal command has given the church more difficulty than all the rest put together: does the term "all nations" include infants? Lest there be pretense, deception, or false advertising here, we must begin by saying that what has not been solved in twenty centuries of debate and research will not be solved with new light in this pocket-sized book. The following remarks are made only to set the book's viewpoint into context.

One must say that those who practice "believers' baptism" (an undifferentiating term, since those who baptize children consider the children too to be believers) have an aspect of the biblical tradition on their side. Far too many Christians of the churches of the Reformation, obedient to the command to study Scripture, find themselves on the "adult baptism" side of the argument for them to be dismissed lightly. Quite obviously the scriptural word is not patent, clear, and unambiguous, or it would be easily discovered. Also, there are some valuable corollaries to the practice of baptizing only adults. Many of the concerns of this book are partly relieved among those who are rigorous about admitting to baptism only those persons sincerely professing an intention to live out its meaning in their lives. Biblical terminology is weighted considerably in favor of the idea of baptism consciously received, though this is in large measure due to the fact that when the New Testament was being written the church was growing chiefly through the accession of adults, and with them of families and whole households.

The discussion here, then, is not intended to prove that the Bible clearly commands baptism of infants, but to discuss the problems which result for those who believe that infants are indeed involved and implied. But the integrity of the book demands an accounting of at least some of the reasons why the writer goes along with the catholic tradition of majority-Christianity.

First, the whole view of baptism implied here is not only compatible with but actually draws strength from the practice of infant baptism. If baptism is part of what God does, not of what man does, if it is God's Word that shapes, creates, reforms, reaches out, acts, and enacts, then the priority does not fall on what man consciously brings. Logically and chronologically the gift of God in baptism precedes what man takes out of it. In baptism it is Christ who brings the child, holds it in his arms, and receives it as a member of his body. The gathered and confessing congregation is a tangible evidence of this action if it really believes that in its forgiven life it is, here in the midst of the world, the very body of Christ. This view of the nature of baptism precommits one to the possibilities of infant baptism.

Second, because of the richness of promise associated with baptism and because of what the inspiring Holy Spirit of God would surely know about an obedient church's response to such a gift, one would almost expect biblical strictures *against* baptizing little children if the promise of baptism were not intended for all persons in all nations who would be baptized and also walk in their baptism.

Third, the whole attitude of Jesus as pictured in the synoptic Gospels conditions us to understand the early church's practice of infant baptism. The Gospel read by many evangelical churches as a child is baptized reminds us that Jesus received infants, blessed them, and used

24

them as models not for "the church of the future" but for the kingdom of the present. Without ever telling the child to take on an adult's faith, he would repeatedly tell the adult to take on the child's faith in its many characteristics of dependence.

Again, the fragment in St. Matthew's Gospel which discusses "all nations" would be the place where exclusive clauses would be expected. Go and baptize whom? Adults? Those over eighteen? Adolescents? Those over twelve? Those who have reached the age of reason? (What is the age of reason?) All these are arguments from silence, I am well aware. But since both sides have to argue from silence, this by itself is not a sufficient criticism.

There are positive glimpses in the New Testament that tend to substantiate the practice of infant baptism or at least call in question some of the objections to it. Some adults were baptized who could hardly have stepped beyond the smallest child's understanding of baptism— picture the surge to the waters at Pentecost, the Ethiopian eunuch's jump into the river, the basin-providing Philippian jailer. Few of the prerequisites that we associate with a fuller-informed response were present in such instances. On more than one occasion the writer of the Book of Acts goes out of his way to show that whole households of people were baptized rather abruptly— even in the middle of the night. These people—the centurion named Cornelius, the Philippian jailer—were military people or civil servants who could be expected to have families and clans of size and, in such households, reasonable entourages of servants. Here and there a rather small child may well have belonged to the household. The citing of these biblical instances is nothing new, and in this space none of them could be expected to be convincing to the people who practice adult baptism alone. In the coming years more veils will probably be torn from the mysteries surrounding not only the theology but, more important, the history of the earliest baptisms.

Typical of such revealing studies, but by no means the last word, is an important work by Joachim Jeremias of Göttingen University in Germany (*Infant Baptism in the First Four Centuries* [Westminster, 1961]). Modest about the biblical evidence and thus not making fantastic claims for a clear-cutness that does not exist, Jeremias pursues the inquiry as far as we now can into the shadows of the earliest church's response. He is particularly impressed by the fact that only two theologians in the first four centuries have left traces of mistrust or rejection of infant baptism. One of these is Tertullian, who in *De Baptismo* asks for delay in the baptizing of the children of pagan parents; but Tertullian coupled this reservation with another: exceptions could be made for emergency. The other witness to express reservations concerning infant baptism was Gregory of Nazianzus, who wanted baptism postponed until the child was three years old. Even more important, notes Jeremias, is the fact that even those two solitary witnesses offered no enduring theological reason for their position. Tertullian based his reservations on the idea of the innocence of children, which made unnecessary the forgiveness which baptism brings (a view held by few Christian thinkers today). He was also worried about overburdening in a hostile, pagan environment the Christian godparents who spoke on behalf of the children. Gregory's concern was that the children should "take in something of the mystery," a welcome but not necessarily biblical motive. In general, those who expressed the earliest reservations about infant baptism were influenced, says Jeremias, "by a magical understanding of baptism," an understanding which has *not* been shared by the modern interpreters who would restrict baptism exclusively to adults.

Additional bits of evidence are adduced by Jeremias and other recent scholars. Some of it is drawn from the growing archeological evidence on monuments and scrolls. Still other scholars, accepting an early date for the Jewish custom of baptizing proselytes, suggest that this practice would have preconditioned the Jewish audiences of Jesus and of his disciples to assume infant baptism. The fact that circumcision (which occurred on an infant's eighth day) was replaced by baptism in Jewish-Christian circles may also indicate that infant baptism was assumed from the first. Readers who wish to pursue the inquiry on historical grounds are advised to consult Jeremias' book; it will also serve as a guide into the literature opposing his own viewpoint.

We must return now to our prime concern, namely, the problems which result for the vast majority of Christians who do baptize infants. How do they carry out the lifelong implications of that command which still seeks to make disciples of the baptized as surely as it first sought to make baptized of the disciples? How does one understand, profit from, and use his own baptism? First a final word, however, on the topic of these past few pages: Christians who witness to "one baptism" should not despair—or bear too much scorn from the world—over the fact of their division on this matter of infant baptism. As they seek more truth and light from Scripture and history and theology, and as they speak and learn together around the tables of Christian gathering, they may be led to fresh answers. Meanwhile, their disagreement, stemming from a common desire to see that neither too many people nor too few are baptized, is actually a tribute— in a world that sorely needs such evidences—to the seriousness with which they take Christ's command to baptize all nations. Christians are concerned to see afresh how this water comprehended in God's command is—

. . . CONNECTED WITH GOD'S WORD . . .

Here "Word" need not be regarded in an exclusive, minimal sense. The Reformers, in the interest of clarity and conviction on one point, were often wont to do this. While it adds strength to one aspect of a position, it does not satisfy the thirst for biblical fullness which a different time demands. So in the Lord's Supper, the "Word" which made a sacrament of bread and wine could be restricted to the Word of institution. True, that was and remains decisive. In Christian baptism, the "Word" that is associated with the water is first and foremost the command of Christ and the trinitarian invocation.

But to the Reformers—and certainly also in the Bible— "Word" meant more. Primarily, it meant what the Bible explicitly calls "the Word," Jesus Christ. The sacraments demand a sense of Christ being present with his activity and his words in the midst of natural elements and the believing community of Christians. As a parallel, "Word" meant the activity and "voice" of God in the Old Testament law and prophets, when God would lay bare his holy arm—to use one of the concrete pictures—or when God uttered his voice and the earth trembled. Thus, derivatively, "the Word" meant the whole of the Scriptures. Christians regard the total context and evidence of Scripture as underscoring the baptismal command and promise. The Word of God formed and then defined the chaos; the Word of God *in Christ* upholds all things by its power; the Word of God parted the waters of the sea, loosed the Flood and then caused it to recede, convinced Job, spoke in whirlwind and conscience, moved John the Baptist, and was present in the baptized Christ. So goes the biblical witness.

Today's baptismal water is still connected with that Word. The Word, says Luther, is everything. Without it—and no Christian would deny this—the water is nothing and baptism does not exist. Without the Word of promise the water would be a baby's bath water or a maid's cooking water, something that can be drawn from the tap and poured out upon the ground. With the Word it is not used to bottle the baptized person to keep him hermetically sealed off from the world and secure for eternity; it is rather poured out into that very world wherein the Christian is to walk after his baptism. Apart from the Word of promise and the faith which grasps the promise it is "simply water"—by now that point should be clear—H_2O in a too-neat silver bowl.

The term "Word of God" means that in the law and the prophets, in Jesus Christ, and in the apostles, God personally addresses man. Here the fatherly heart of God, mirrored in Jesus Christ, is actually revealed. The veils which hide an aloof, distant, and unknowable God are withdrawn, and in the midst of a world of flesh and blood, dirt and water, God acts through visible and tangible means. Here is a channel of grace, a word made visible, a sacrament. "Do this!" and receive Christ's benefits. "Go and baptize" and make Christ's disciples.

In the Book of Acts the baptismal water's connection with the Word of God is apparent in the trinitarian invocation, particularly as that was focused in "the name" of Jesus Christ. Baptism's connection with the Word of God depends in large measure on its involvement with this name. Again and again in the Book of Acts it is evident that baptism was in this name, by faith in this name. Acts 4:12 sets the apostolic stamp on the reason: "There is salvation in no one else, for there is no other name under heaven given among men by which we must be saved." In the biblical world a "name" represented all that a person was, his character and his qualities. (Advertisers' devotion to the "image" of a brand name is our best modern parallel for this understanding.) The name of God *was* God; baptism in the name of Jesus was baptism into Christ. "Connection with the Word" thus means that baptism relates a person to the whole plan of God: in the case of Christ's baptism, "This is my beloved Son"; and in the case of the Christian's baptism, "He that believeth and is baptized shall be saved." This is why the ancient baptismal commands are of considerable importance to moderns who stand in the same need.

If the reality and the personhood of God are implied in the name of Jesus Christ, then the trinitarian formula that has grown out of the baptismal command takes on new life. Unitarians have derided this phrase, claiming that the invocation of "Father, Son, and Holy Spirit" means Christians are baptized in the name of "an abstraction, a man, and a metaphor." The Christian replies that "in the name of the Father" relates his baptism to the whole of creation—and its water; "in the name of the Son" calls to mind the whole personal relation of the baptized community to God in Christ; and "in the name of the Holy Spirit" means that God takes the initiative, turning the letter into spirit and creating the church. Indeed this fullness of meaning is surely implicit already in the summary formula which concludes and climaxes the first Gospel. What is that Word of God to which the water of baptism is connected?

> *It is that which our Lord Jesus Christ spake, as it is recorded in the last chapter of Matthew, verse 19: "Go ye, and teach all nations, baptizing them in the name of the Father, and of the Son, and of the Holy Ghost."*

What Does Baptism Do?

Baptism is the gospel in miniature, portrayed, lived out, enacted. And the gospel is promise. And promise, in biblical language, is not merely the offer of a gift on the part of God but the very gift itself imparted with that offer. The faith that receives, is nourished by, and relates to baptism clings to the promise which centers in the reality of the forgiveness of sins. This reality produces the only kind of joy that the Christian needs to seek or should seek.

The person today who wishes to explore the meaning of the water of life is handicapped by the fact that he and the world in which he lives do not seem to be asking the question which baptism answers. He may be experiencing relative health, comfort, prosperity, and security. The furthest thing from his mind on many a morning is any pressing weight of sin. How then can he understand the baptismal gift of freedom from sin, a gift he does not need? He may be the psychological type often described as "healthy-minded" whose sins are simply not at the forefront of his imagination or consciousness. He may be an intellectually secure believer who has been told—and has assented to the proposition—that God loves him and forgives sins, and who therefore does not have to think about it any more. He may have undertaken the once difficult but eventually easy process of dulling his own conscience and interest in God's Word of judgment. Possibly, though, he does have moments when he is slightly aware of a restlessness within himself, which a clever preacher can convince him is a hunger for God and for forgiveness. At times he may even experience the loneliness of the unforgiven and the unacceptable; but this usually occurs because some other human holds something against him, not because he is conscious of having offended God.

So, as a child of his times, he perhaps admires the Psalmist who made his couch a bed of tears in agony over his guilt, but he simply cannot identify himself with that situation. He may undertake psychological and psychoanalytic research into the mind of the young Luther to find out why the Reformer agonized so much over the question, "How can I find a gracious God?" but he pays good money to hide the realities which could put him in such a fix. He may marvel at the modern Roman Catholic wise man, G. K. Chesterton, who on being asked why he joined the church replied, "To get rid of my sins." But then he wonders and is even mildly critical about the selfishness of it all: Does the church exist just so I can get rid of my sins? What about my brother? What about an abandoned world? We are here for all the others: What are all the others here for? Thus it is that the man of today hears of a cure to a disease he does not recognize.

Later we shall see what baptism can do to help such a person undertake the self-scrutiny necessary to receive its gifts—for baptism *is* repentance. For the moment it is sufficient—and important—to point out that the person in question cannot lightly be put aside. There is no reason for him to invent psychological problems he does not now have. The Christian gospel is intended to give him peace, and it may be that at least some of his peace—however superficial its edges—does flow out of a Christian center. The gospel has done some of its work. Further, he cannot be blamed for being born in a time when only the neurotically anxious seem to be able to sustain a sense of real guilt (do only *they* believe in God or believe that God cares?). It is also true that the untroubled modern can be helped by an act of translation. Forgiveness does not mean a mere psychological judgment or adjustment. It means a new circumstance, a new stance of man before God, a new thing, a new creation.

Our modern friend then—and this may be autobiographical for most of us today—has the familiar problem of not having a problem at all, or at least of not recognizing the problem. In C. S. Lewis' well-known exegesis of the Prayer Book phrase, "We are miserable offenders," man recognizes the problem of not recognizing that he is miserable. The passengers on two trains speeding toward each other on the same tracks may be reading a magazine, or dozing over a drink, or laughing boisterously. They do not feel miserable. As an objective statement of their condition, however, they *are* in fact quite miserable and action must be taken. Baptism addresses itself to this kind of situation. Happening to most people when they are children, baptism is not "felt" as part of an adult experience. Not only is the water long since dried, but the napkin is rotted and the church building even forgotten or burned down. Yet baptism is designed for the real circumstance of the man: he is in fact very much in need of God. Perhaps his greatest problem is that he is born in a time which obscures the problem; he has been given a malleable conscience.

For his righteousness does *not* exceed the righteousness of the scribes and Pharisees around him. He has not extended the cup of cold water, visited the imprisoned, clothed the cold, sheltered the shelterless, fed the hungry— and thus has not served Christ. So the kingdom of God is not his without help. His ethical situation, even in its respectability, makes him an outcast. Yet baptism can help him. It can help even the good man. Cornelius was described in Acts 10 as an "upright and God-fearing man, who is well spoken of by the whole Jewish nation." His prayer had been heard and his alms were remembered. Yet Peter commanded baptism "in the name of Jesus Christ" and it was done.

Baptism works the forgiveness of sins; indeed baptism is the forgiveness of sins. "It overcomes and takes away sin" (Luther's *Large Catechism,* IV, 83). The water of the old creation and the Word of the new achieve the new creation in man. Sin is washed away according to one picture; the sinner is drowned and dies according to the other. In either case the old self is shattered, annihilated, mortified, killed. Man does not earn his place or work his way up in the kingdom. He is a helpless, sputtering, crying infant with empty hands and uninformed head and no report card at all with which to impress God. Thus does baptism begin. He is the kneeling, listening man, again with empty hands in search of a clean heart and a right spirit. Of him God can make something new. This time newness comes not the easy way as the oldest story has it: by the breath of God, out of nothing. Instead it comes the hard way: by the death of Christ, and out of the sinner.

Once this is seen, even in its first implications, the center of baptism has been properly located. The forgiveness of sins becomes the glowing core, the center out of which the full Christian life will flow. At baptism the sign of the cross is made over the person; he is invited to enjoy the fellowship of the resurrection and to share the burden of Christ's suffering.

What he receives is not a different grace, or a different kind of grace. He receives the same grace in a form consistent with his need. Jesus, Peter, and the other apostles take the element of water and use it to bring Christ's benefits and the righteousness of God. There is perhaps no better illustration of this formal consistency than the statement of the great Pavlova who, after a demanding dance, was asked to interpret its meaning in words. "My God," she replied, "do you think I would have danced it if I could have said it?" It is not that God has to use this particular means because he is too limited to devise any other: he does it because it is the way to get across to man the fact of his cleansing, his death-to-life dance, his forgiveness, his freedom.

Baptism as the forgiveness of sins does not make man into a solitary saint, a hermit. Forgiveness always occurs in the fellowship of creatures; the baptized person is now a member of the people of God. In this day of the recovery of the laity we often hear that baptism is the act of ordination into the laity, and that a clergyman is merely a set-aside, professional member of the laity (*laos*-people). It is true that baptism is the charter for the universal priesthood of believers with its privilege and responsibility. The baptized man is now free to be an intercessor, one who can love his neighbor while in a kneeling posture, and pray for others' forgiveness. Yet the idea of his participation as an intercessor, his activity as a new priest, a member of God's people, should not be used—as is easily done—to wrench baptism away from its center in the forgiveness received.

Here again the assumptions behind infant baptism can be of help, for in such baptism the passivity of the recipient is pictured well. Later, when the child has to struggle to be what he really is, least and greatest in the kingdom, this passivity is not so apparent. But on *this* morning he is "being baptized"—an act that can only be expressed in the passive mood. It is this receiving posture which helps to keep him from regarding the cultic act, or the mystery of initiation, or the meticulousness with which

35

he carries out a command as the ladder on which he hoists himself up into heaven. Contributing to the same end is the humbling that he also receives in other ways. For he has manifold needs, and a struggle is constantly going on. Baptism addresses itself to that too. For while it works forgiveness of sins, it also—

. . . DELIVERS FROM DEATH AND THE DEVIL . . .

In biblical language these are the classic enemies. Today the first of these is too vivid for us to let it become real and the second is too real for us to let it become vivid. Both are enemies of God's plan for the good of man. The Bible tells us less than we would like to know about the origin of these enemies, and more than we need to know about coping with them. That "more" is baptism.

The language of deliverance is being recovered for baptism today. Chiefly it is associated with the memories of the crossing of the Red Sea. Baptism is what cultural anthropologists would call a "rite of passage." But it is not merely a passing into a new age of life or a new understanding of that age. It is rather a deliverance from the end of life and from the nagging assault on the good in every moment of life. It was the waters of the sea which swallowed the enemies of God's people of old. Luther's *Large Catechism* uses a different metaphor but an apt one: "Now, here in baptism there is brought free to every man's door just such a priceless medicine which swallows up death and saves the lives of all men" (IV, 43). Because baptism is Word and water, "body and soul shall be saved and live forever: the soul through the Word in which it believes, the body because it is united with the soul and apprehends baptism in the only way it can. No greater jewel, therefore, can adorn our body and soul than baptism, for through it we obtain perfect holiness and salvation, which no other kind of life and no work on earth can acquire" (IV, 46).

Baptism is the use of one "death" (recall the picture of drowning?) to kill off another. A minister bringing the water of life to a child through a plastic aperture in the incubator knows how vividly such a baptism outshines the bright, antiseptic, stained-glass kind performed at church. For here in the hospital the child is clearly hovering between life and death; he may possibly be snatched from the jaws of death to live, but he is certainly—by the promise of God—being snatched from the jaws of Death to Live. When such a child survives it is a joy to see its later vitality and vibrancy against the background of its early hours, and to realize with the parents how few are the traces of its feeble past. Such an experience is a parallel to that which occurs in every baptism: a snatching from the jaws of death, a deliverance through water.

While death is a problem only at the very beginning and end of mortal experience, before baptism and again prior to the autopsy, the devil is a constant problem. The personal opposition to the plan of God is intensified in the baptized. As Christ went from his baptism to the mount of temptation, so it is pre-eminently the maturing Christian who experiences the power of temptation. For in baptism he has "put on Christ" and is found "in Christ." It is the Christ in him that is tempted again. Once this is recognized, the power of God is unfolded in new and fuller measure. The ultimate victory is already in sight because baptism also—

. . . CONFERS EVERLASTING SALVATION . . .

It is to the question of salvation that baptism addresses itself. The first gift of baptism, the forgiveness of sins, is not an end in itself; it is a means. Man is forgiven *in order that* he can live the free, responsible, and joyful

37

life—in order that he can be saved everlastingly. It is important to locate properly the emphasis on salvation.

Much of the current problem over the use of baptism derives from a misplaced emphasis with respect to the idea of being saved. The water of baptism is not an aqueous solution for bottling and preserving the Christian until such time as he is shipped off to the kingdom. It is rather the water from which he rises, through which he is delivered, by which he is cleansed. Most of the curiosity concerning baptism's mysteries grew out of a conception which postpones its effects into an afterlife. We are hardly curious at all about the meaning and implications of baptism for the baptized and for those living now in history. But we are extremely curious about the unbaptized and those living in eternity: Is baptism necessary for salvation? Is a child who dies without baptism lost? These are typical questions, and they are understandable too, particularly among parents of an unbaptized child who has died. These frequently agonizing inquiries are not to be minimized or shrugged off. Yet it must be said that they arise in part out of a climate in which Christian life and teaching generally, and the practice of baptism in particular, are seen in terms of a misplaced emphasis. In a sense they begin at the wrong end. They are much like the questions concerning election and predestination. They presuppose that humans are capable of peering into the naked divine majesty to search out an answer that has not been clearly revealed. Known is the fact that a child dies. Unknown is the disposition God will make of the matter.

The movement of the biblical answer, however, comes in the opposite direction. The Old Testament, for example, shows precious little interest in questions concerning *my* personal destiny in the afterlife. It focuses singly on the character, the love, the complete trustworthiness of God.

God is not the God of the dead but of the living. In the New Testament when taunters asked Jesus which of seven husbands a very durable widow would be married to in the afterlife, and when skeptics asked Paul to describe the kinds of bodies men would have in the next life, they both parried the question. It is impossible to answer! We are creatures of time and space; we are limited to God's answers in the here and now. Salvation begins now. Eternal life is a quality that breaks in already in the very midst of this world, as the writer of the Fourth Gospel repeatedly insists.

This means that the Christian faith is not just a religion of salvation, a cult (like the mystery cults of its early years) which sees this world to be unimportant. It does not exist just to snatch people away from this life and ship them off to some future life that alone is important. Rather it thrusts men back with eternal life into the midst of this earthly life.

If the church today were more concerned with this matter of eternal life in the here and now its ethics and theology would improve, but even more its popular piety would take on a different character. It would be led to answer more confidently these popular and puzzling questions about eternity even before they are asked. What about the unbaptized child then? Proceed from the known to the unknown. The command of God is known. No conceivable answer dare relax the seriousness with which God demands that Christians live out his ordinances. No glib assurances should be sold on the market place as tickets to others' complacency and neglect. Otherwise the promises of God with baptism cannot come through. Now, keeping the full seriousness of the command in view, proceed again from the known to the unknown. The promise of God is known: God would have all men to be saved. The thief on the cross in the Gospels' account

was assured of salvation, having received no baptism
except a death shared with his Savior. Again, the Word
of God is not bound. Again, God does not reveal himself
as one who capriciously goes out of his way to cause
suffering or annihilation; he is a God of grace and of love.

The best therapy with which one can comfort the
parents of a dead unbaptized child is to point to the
character of God, not to a guidebook of purgatories,
limbos, or Abraham's bosoms. The question about the
unbaptized child is one that should be answered with
extreme reservation and care in general, in the abstract,
but with extreme warmth and confidence in the particular,
in the concrete instance: God is known in the wounds
of Christ; what does this known-ness mean to you, mother
and father?

By analogy other questions related to this one can be
analyzed. (As to what happens to the child born in Tibet,
this is the kind of question that must be discussed in an
entirely different context. Until students of the Christian
gospel and of comparative religion solve the question of
"a justifying God where Christ is not known" the authors
of short books on baptism can hardly undertake to deal
with the subject. Discipline commends the procedure of
discussing baptism only within the scope of its place and
meaning in the believing community.)

Only unbelief condemns. "One can become righteous
by faith," writes Luther, "without the bodily reception
of the sacraments, so long as one does not despise them."
And again, "Christ says: 'He who believes and is baptized
will be saved; but he who does not believe will be con-
demned' (Mark 16:16). He shows us in this word that
faith is such a necessary part of the sacrament that it
can save even without the sacrament, and for this reason
he did not add: 'He who does not believe, and is not
baptized.'" (American edition of *Luther's Works* [Phila-

delphia: Muhlenberg, 1958-59], XXXII, 15; XXXVI, 67.)

The important thing is for Christians to see what salvation "everlastingly" means in the life that is lived now, in which they are now given room (the idea of spaciousness is implicit in the Hebrew terms for salvation) to breathe and to serve.

The promises of forgiveness, deliverance, and salvation in baptism are extended to—

. . . ALL WHO BELIEVE, AS THE WORD AND PROMISE OF GOD DECLARE.

These words of Luther were written—we must repeatedly remind ourselves—against a background of a magical conception of the sacraments. Faith is always connected with the sacraments, faith *in* God, faith *that* he will enact his promises. This faith is expressed by the whole community of Christians, often through the godparent or sponsor who answers for a child as his "vicar" or representative. The custom of having godparents in the baptism of people too young to answer for themselves goes at least as far back as the third century. Older people have always, after instruction, expressed personally the faith in the promise held by the whole community. Those who believe and speak are responding to the Word; for faith is an "acoustical affair" with which, in the Word, God bridges the infinite distance between himself and the man he would win to himself. And what are these words and promises of God?

Those which our Lord Jesus Christ spake, as they are recorded in the last chapter of Mark, verse 16: "He that believeth and is baptized, shall be saved; but he that believeth not, shall be damned."

The flesh of Jesus, the incarnation of the Word of God, is the place where men either stumble and fall, or rise to newness of life. When Christ is formed in us, there is "everlasting salvation." This is the gift of baptism.

How Can Water Do This?

*It is not the water indeed that produces these effects,
but the Word of God which accompanies and is connected
with the water, and our faith which relies on the Word
of God connected with the water. For the water, without
the Word of God, is simply water and no baptism. But
when connected with the Word of God, it is a baptism;
that is, a gracious water of life and a "washing of regeneration" in the Holy Ghost, as St. Paul says to Titus,
in the third chapter, verses 5-8:*

> *"According to his mercy he saved us, by the
> washing of regeneration and renewing of the
> Holy Ghost; which he shed on us abundantly
> through Jesus Christ our Savior; that being
> justified by his grace, we should be made heirs
> according to the hope of eternal life. This is a
> faithful saying."*

The first portion of this statement can serve as a
summary of what has preceded, for much of what it
implies has been discussed briefly already. The statement
itself is indicative of how carefully the church of the
Reformation tried to keep alive two poles in its answer
to the question: "What is baptism?" On the one hand
it was careful not to fall into the trap of overmaterializing
the sacrament as it had seen Western Catholicism do in
the late medieval period, when the Word and faith seemed
to play no significant part. On the other hand it was
cautious with respect to interpretations of the "left-wing
of the Reformation" which so emphasized the spiritual,

43

the verbal, the intellectual, the nonmaterial that the water of baptism was vaporized into insignificance, and the ordinance and promise of God connected with the water in effect reduced to nothing. Meanwhile it was careful to insist that the faith which saw the promise in the water and heard it in the Word should not be regarded as an achievement of man, a claim upon God.

What now needs to be explored cursorily is the assertion that the water of life is a "washing of regeneration," to use the expression of the letter to Titus. We have already spoken about the existence of washings, lustrations, initiation ceremonies, cleansings, and baths. What is still to be pointed to is the connection in the Christian context between these washings and the gift of renewal of the Holy Ghost. Just as the water is shed on the baptized person, so the Holy Ghost is "shed on us abundantly." The comparison recalled to the letter writer the gift of the Holy Ghost in the baptism by water and by fire at Pentecost, as well, no doubt, as the appearance of the dove recorded in the Gospel tradition. The Holy Spirit as sanctifier was seen to be the purifier and purger. He could use fire, he could use suffering, he could use tongues. The Fourth Gospel records in chapter 3 a conversation between Jesus and Nicodemus in which it is made clear that spirit and water are to be connected not only in the Old Testament but also—as Spirit and Water —in the new. Through this gift the writer to Titus said man was "justified by grace" and "made heir" of the hope of eternal life. In other words, in baptism the church is born; or, the mothering church receives another child to her bosom. Baptism is also a calling, enlightening, gathering, and sanctifying act. The association of light with the darkness that preceded it in the ceremony of the Easter Vigil certainly carries symbolism of the flame of the Spirit. It is in the awareness of the continued presence of the Holy Spirit that confirmation is related to baptism.

Confirmation is ill-defined in the Protestant tradition. Perhaps this is fortunate. It is a salutary rite of the church because it provides opportunity for instruction and the undertaking of personal resolves. But most attempts to define it too precisely as a ratification of baptism, a personal reasserting of former baptismal vows to "make them mine," issue in a failure to preserve the uniqueness of the baptismal promise. They imply an incompleteness about baptism to which the New Testament does not admit. Suffice it to say that when an infant is baptized some sort of pledge must be exacted from those who bring him that he will be taught the Ten Commandments, the Creed, the Lord's Prayer, brought to the house of God, and permitted to grow into the form of Christ which is his gift at baptism. The Holy Spirit guides the entire process, which is in the hands of the church, the community in whose faith the child is first presented and received for his second birth, his new birth, his washing of regeneration and renewal.

How does one move from the faith of the community-of-faith to the personal faith implied in baptism? The lack of definition concerning confirmation can be a help here. Faith can of course be confirmed on a particular day in a particular rite after particular preparation. But more important: How is one *regularly* confirmed in this faith? What is this faith? And what is its connection with baptism? When these questions are asked, baptism appears in a different light. The faith of the church, the faith which is a gift in baptism, is in one sense complete and sufficient; there is nothing that maturity and intellectuality can add to it. In another sense, however, as layers of complexity in life are added day by day through all the years, so too will layers of complexity be found to accrue in faith's response.

If faith means dependence—the absence of anxiety about the morrow, the active or passive repose of one in the destiny of the Other, the security of the faltering hand inside the strong hand—then baptismal faith has already said all there is to say. The childlike becomes the model: any faith which does not share this quality cannot matter in the kingdom of God. The humble spirit is fed on the milk of the Word, on the promise connected with the water. With advancing maturity the growth in wisdom and stature brings about crises and quests for new understanding. It is the apparent contradiction within faith—at once already complete and yet in need of fulfillment—that forces evangelical Christians to speak in somewhat circular fashion.

Baptism gives birth to faith, we say, yet faith in turn is a requisite to the response in baptism. The sacrament gives eternal salvation to all who believe, yet the faith of the baptized is in turn seen to make him worthy. This circle dare not be interrupted by concerns over the merit of the baptized one. The faith he brings to the act and to the daily renewal of the act is not credited, as it were, on a divine report card. Faith *receives* baptism, it does not constitute it. For this reason faith, in this context, usually can be described more as a "being grasped" than a "grasping," though the active mood is necessarily implied.

This view of faith serves as a divider over against the view of faith which demands adult baptism only. In a sense we might say that the varying attitudes toward faith do not flow out of the practice or nonpractice of infant baptism. On the contrary, it is the particular definition of faith that results in a certain kind of baptism. Where faith is dependent on the competence of the individual soul, where it is the fruit of an effort of man's will, where it is in part an intellectual achievement, maturity of years is regarded understandably as a requisite. But where Christian faith is a belief in the God who upholds me apart from my constant wakeful activity and achievement, the recipient of grace walks in childlike faith. Faith receives and faith is the result. Faith is awakened and strengthened by baptism and faith renews baptism in daily life. It is actually God who acts decisively in initiating the life of faith.

Gustav Aulén has pointed out that with this view of faith as God's activity and not as the mere product of man's soul-competence, evangelical Christians would quite logically baptize infants even if it were not directly a part of the original command and most ancient practice. Only in such a practice is the divine initiative in the life of faith made bold and luminous. Waking or sleeping, the Christian belongs to his Lord. At one and the same time both justified and a sinner, the Christian returns to the faith that was his promise in the beginning.

But faith is not only the grand undergirding of life. It is also a matter of obedience. Again and again the New Testament speaks of the maturing faith as an obedient response while one moves "from faith to faith." Faith as obedience, however, is not faith as merit or as work or as achievement. The believer is freed from all such burdens. Obedient faith is simply a joyous confessing faith; it is a faith "in" someone. Obedient confessing faith contains a "knowing," an "intellectuality" if you will (as those who baptize only adults contend), but it is freed from concern over how *much* knowledge and how *much* achievement one brings. To know is not so important as to "be known" of God (Gal. 4:9; I Cor. 13:12).

Finally, such faith contains an element of hope that

47

has already been implied at baptism in the intercession of the responding community. Baptismal faith is confident. It points to the end of an age, a creation, indeed a new creation, a new life in the new age.

What Does Baptism Mean for Life?

BAPTISM SIGNIFIES THAT THE OLD ADAM IN US IS TO
BE DROWNED AND DESTROYED . . .

For the first time in its discussion of baptism the *Small Catechism* uses the term "signifies." Up to this point the pictorial aspect of baptism has been largely suppressed, and hence much of the biblical context left behind. This was done so that we might single-mindedly pursue not what baptism portrays but what baptism actually is, offers, and does. However, baptism *is* also a death and resurrection, a death and resurrection which is vividly portrayed in an historic form of the baptismal act, namely, immersion. The body is submerged under the water so that a death, entombment, or drowning is lived out and experienced. Then there is a deliverance, a rising, a portrayed resurrection.

Baptism is thus connected with what historians of the religions of ancient times would call "the fate of the cult-deity." Most of the religions that surrounded early Christianity, particularly in the Greco-Roman world, followed the rhythms of their deities' lives. The Old Testament had nothing to do with this imagery. The New Testament allows for it in the matter of sharing the sufferings and glory of Jesus Christ, in whom the fullness of God was seen to dwell bodily. He died and was buried; he rose. In baptism the Christian undertakes the same geometric curve, a surrogate for the experience of depth and height, defeat and victory. Those who dogmatically insist on baptism by complete immersion—as the Bible does not—certainly have this picture in their favor and we could wish that immersions were more frequent in the evangelical and catholic traditions of the Western church so that the reality implied would be more vivid.

When we speak of man's "old Adam" we mean all that he is. Included are his sins and virtues, his injustices and righteousnesses, his body and soul, spirit, reason, faculties—chop him up as you will. All these, seen apart from Christ, represent man's total need before God. This is the self that must die if the new self is to be born. Baptism was and is such an ultimate action. The drowning and destruction is to occur—

. . . BY DAILY SORROW AND REPENTANCE . . .

The whole Christian life has frequently been defined as repentance. If we would still regard it as such we must remember that repenting is not a masochistic, self-centered, narcissistic act in which a man enjoys his miseries. It is rather a God-directed, Christ-centered, selfless act in which a man enjoys the divine gift. While the New Testament imagery does include a sense of being wrenched from the luxuries and securities of one's past, it concentrates mainly on the joy of newness: God *gives* the gift of repentance. The old is purged for only one purpose, so the new can enter. The wedding garment is put on only in order that the wedding can actually begin as the bridegroom comes.

Daily repentance involves "contrition" (a positive, "godly" sorrow) under the law of God and by faith in the gospel. This is in effect a daily return to baptism. "Repentance," says Luther, "is really nothing else than baptism. What is repentance but an earnest attack on the old man and an entering upon a new life? If you live in repentance, therefore, you are walking in baptism, which not only announces this new life but also produces,

begins, and promotes it. . . . Repentance, therefore, is
nothing else than a return and approach to baptism, to
resume and practice what had earlier been begun but
abandoned" (*Large Catechism,* IV, 74-79).

The Christian examines himself not "in general" but
in particular, in the light of the Ten Commandments. He
sees his shortcomings over against the commands of God.
He permits his life to be reoriented in the aspect of his
baptism. He surrenders his old self—

. . . TOGETHER WITH ALL SINS AND EVIL LUSTS . . .

Sometimes sin is pictured in the Bible as the whole
relation of the "old Adam" to God. Sometimes it is pictured as accidental additions to the life of man, some
things that can be numbered, counted, and conquered.
We are told that when sins, lusts, and temptations both-
ered Luther he would scrawl, "I am baptized," as a reminder to himself of his new true identity, as a shield
against assault and a request for divine aid.

Such a defense makes sense only in the life of one
who daily practices walking in repentance and in his baptism—otherwise it is nothing but an incantation, a magic
phrase. It "works" only in the life of the person who
receives regularly at the Lord's table the nourishment of
the other sacrament. It grows in effectiveness especially
in the life of him who is learning to engage in self-
appraisal through the Ten Commandments and to ap-
preciate the armament which is the Lord's Prayer (Lead
us not into temptation but deliver us from the evil one).
It is of greatest help to the man who is conscious of the
fact that he has been buried with Christ, and that God
has put on him the white robe of Christ's gifts. In such
a person something new can really happen. He will
understand—

... THAT AGAIN THE NEW MAN SHOULD DAILY COME
FORTH AND RISE ...

The early Christians oriented their churches toward
the rising sun. They saw their daily rising from sleep as a
conformation to Christ's resurrection. They changed their
holy day to the Lord's Day to celebrate his rising. They
baptized most frequently on the Vigil of Easter, or on
Easter Day, or in the Easter season, so that the coming
forth and rising would be most vivid and meaningful. They
understood that it was the total personality, not just some
disembodied "soul" or "spirit" which had been drenched
and was to rise. The whole body was to be used to God's
purpose; it could not, for example, be joined to a pros-
titute because it was already the temple of the Holy Spirit.
Death and yesterday were behind.

The new man nourished by the water of life is part of
the body of Christ. The rising involved in baptism is a
social activity; it places one into solidarity with all others
who share it. The old aeon, the old creation has passed
away for all who are members one of another. Paul used
vivid imagery to depict life in this "body." He spoke of
membranes, joints, ligaments, and lesser members. This
concreteness was most evident in what he wrote to the
Corinthians concerning a certain strange ephemeral practice of theirs. We know little of what he meant when he
spoke of being "baptized for the dead" (I Cor. 15:29).
Evidently some of the people at Corinth believed they
could be baptized vicariously as representatives of others
who had preceded them in death. The practice, men-
tioned only in this one instance, was no doubt corrected;
at any rate it disappeared quite early despite the temptations of its appeal. What is important in the context of
our discussion is that Paul was so urgently intent upon
detailing the concreteness of the baptized Christian's life
in the membraned-jointed-ligamented body of Christ that

for the moment he could even overlook in passing the necessary housecleaning implied in this particular short-lived practice.

Baptism still involves people in the whole body of Christ. It may mean participation in the routines of a parish, suffering under a nameless burden, carrying on in unaesthetic and personally distasteful surroundings, loving the unlikeable, accepting the unacceptable. But the test remains in the concreteness and visibility that the new life daily takes. Those who rise from their baptismal water delivered and cleansed now carry the wounds of Christ in the midst of the world so that his glory may shine forth. The result of such living is clear: the new man—

. . . SHALL LIVE IN THE PRESENCE OF GOD IN RIGHT-EOUSNESS AND PURITY FOR EVER.

The scriptural statement of this meaning of baptism is the *Catechism's* final word on the subject:

> *St. Paul, in the Epistle to the Romans, chapter 6, verse 4, says: "We are buried with Christ by baptism into death that like as he was raised up from the dead by the glory of the Father, even so we also should walk in newness of life."*

"With Christ." The church of the Reformation, called to different tasks in its first generation, did not accent as much as we moderns must do in our isolated, atomized lives the fact that baptism incorporates us into Christ. Martin Thornton writes, "We are in Christ, not as a pebble in a box but as a branch on a tree." The individualism, autonomy, going-my-own-way, do-it-yourself, busy-busy view of religion that has prevailed in the recent past is a denial of baptism. It is this view that has made necessary all the crusades for church attendance. If a man is in Christ as a branch is in a tree he will be present in all vital expressions of that oneness, such as the regular worship and Communion. If Christ is present and man is not, the oneness is broken. Baptism is a "plural" activity. Perhaps too much stress has been placed on the giving of a name at baptism. *I* already had a name at the time I was baptized. What actually happens is that *we* receive Christ's name at the time ours are written in the book of life.

In the under-and-out of baptism, in its death-and-resurrection we see the grain of wheat that falls into the ground and dies in order to rise and bring forth fruit. Christ is the first fruit. By his resurrection all the rest live daily. It has often been pointed out that in the Pauline writings the term "discipleship" disappears and "baptism" takes its place. Jesus in his word and call, and especially in baptism, is looking less for hearers than for followers, for disciples. "When Jesus Christ calls a man he bids him come and die." But man dies in baptism to live in newness of life. In all this the glory of the Father is seen. It was he who raised Christ. It is he who extends the promise in baptism. And it is he who makes it possible that we also should walk in newness of life.

The term "newness of life" is based on the Ephesian references to the new creation and the new man, and on the Pauline witness to baptism as resurrection in Romans chapter six. As such it bears witness to a new reality and a new mode of conduct, the Christian ethic. Newness always grows out of the forgiven life of faith, which is the pre-eminent gift of baptism. Such life is open to the possibilities of the new day and the new age. It centers in the "new man," successor to the "old man" who in baptism was crucified and put into the grave with Christ. This new man has already tasted the resurrection for he is in the body of Christ, who is the first fruit of the resurrection. In every return to his baptismal promise he is removed from the oldness of sin and the old creation. He has "put off" the former man with the passions and lusts, the bondage to the flesh that was involved.

This radical change is not often recognized in ordinary talk about ethics, in which we hear mostly moralizing advice about somehow being a better person every day. People are commonly asked to refrain from making critical judgments "because there is so much bad in the best of us and so much good in the worst of us." Often this moralizing talk is mistakenly confused with Christian talk. But the moralizers have lost the definition of one world and the joy of another. Their "old man" of evil is defined in terms of the world's view of pessimism: man is quite bad. Their "new man" of good is defined in terms of the world's view of optimism: every day in every way one becomes a bit better. Poised between these weak alternatives, a person is supposed to live his life according to a code or norm established by law; he is to be good and try harder—he is not free!

The new man in Christ is really free; he has put off entirely the former things. Though they will return to gnaw at his freedom whenever he sins, his baptism is the enduring sign and seal of promise. Each time the Holy Spirit enacts a new creation in him he is extricated from moralizing and legalistic tendencies. The "old man" is actually worse than the world thought him to be in comparison with the "new man," and the "new man" bears possibilities the world did not anticipate. Newness of life means that the redeemed people can *look* redeemed, that God's own love can flow through their lives, that his created order can be used by them to new and enduring good.

The application of water to the body in baptism serves

to vivify the Christian witness to resurrection and the new life in the midst of the old world. Baptism is not just directed at souls, at minds and spirits. That which is drowned and buried with Christ is the very body which will be committed to the earth one day as having been created by God, redeemed by Christ, and sanctified by the Holy Spirit. It is a cell in the living body of Christ. It is described as a temple of the Holy Spirit, not to be misused in the world's fashion. The sign of the cross is made over the body that will later be asked to bear the cross, the body which in its resurrected reality is to share the crown of Christ's rewarding life. The whole person (a term which captures much of what the New Testament often means by "body") is involved in Christ's life now.

This newness is a gift in baptism. It is recovered each Easter in faith in the resurrection, each Lord's Day as the sun of the new creation bursts in upon the old, with each concrete return to and recall of the faith which was baptism's gift, and in the joy of forgiveness. Such newness moves bodily out into the world; it enters into the real world, not just some spiritual, abstract, chimerical world. How one acts then becomes decisively important—if the Name is to be known and honored. Faith becomes active in love; love means complete devotion to God and then, as Augustine would say, freedom to "do as you please" in His service.

This newness cannot, of course, be fully realized in the old age, the old creation, the present body. It points to the age to come, which the baptized believer already has but for which one also hopes. The name written in the book of life at baptism causes rejoicing, for this name is sealed with the new covenant in the divine and fulfilled life. In baptism, we are reminded, every Christian has enough to learn and practice to keep him busy all his life. But his historical life does not exhaust the possibility which God has placed in baptism: "And I saw a new heaven and a new earth: for the first heaven and the first earth were passed away" (Rev. 21:1). "And he shewed me a pure river of life, clear as crystal, proceeding out of the throne of God and of the Lamb" (Rev. 22:1). For the song of newness in its full chorus the language of the visionary represents the best effort. One reaches for such a language, almost picturing the new man, seeing the crystal waters, being reminded of his own trip to the Jordan, his own visit to the font, his own foretaste in this world of the new life to come.

Conclusion:
Suggestions for Practice

Several consequences and practical suggestions are now apparent. The Christian life is seen as a life of simplicity, born and nourished in a simple act, baptism. It would seem that while it is desirable to bring the whole biblical imagery to bear on baptism, the sacrament itself should appear in the simplest of contexts. It should be preserved from those who would prettify and enrich worship out of purely aesthetic considerations. A trip to the river would still be the most vivid form, but is not likely to prevail in the immediate future. The primitiveness of the sacrament seems to be integral to its form, and helpful in making it effective later.

Some aspects of this simplicity and directness perhaps involve emphases which the baptizing church may wish to consider. No individual member will be able to effect them, but thought, discussion, and action could flow from a better understanding of baptism generally. For example, since baptism is so closely related to confession, might it not be possible for the churches presently restoring private confession to more regular use to do this in the context of the font, as a vivid reminder of the baptismal character of repentance and of the passivity of man's part in achieving the new life?

The words which remain from the early rites of exorcism which once preceded baptism need reappraisal. Either they should be dropped or more should be done to promote their understanding. An occasional sermon on the setting of demonic temptation and an occasional inquiry into the history of the act could be of help. Without this it would seem that few godparents will have a vivid sense of what it means in the modern world (without the ancient ceremonies of salt or oil or a clear picture of the demonic reality) to "renounce the devil and all his works and all his ways."

In the absence of immersion one could at least explore the possibilities of using as much water as possible, so that the dual aspect of the sacramental reality may be more apparent. If one cannot discreetly dip the infant in the font, he can at least douse it generously. If he cannot portray the drowning through immersion, he can at least portray the washing by a liberal splashing instead of a scant drop on the forehead. He can leave a bit of a mess at the foot of the font and around the neck of the child and not be overly tidy in removing every molecule of moisture.

When an adult is baptized, he should be encouraged to receive the sacrament in public. In an overrun Christian culture, where everyone has "had baptism done" adult baptisms are witnessed too seldom to occasion much thought about the history of the act. To spare adults embarrassment they are usually sneaked off into private chambers. Those who have been talked into the public act can testify that, once the case of nerves was over, they were grateful for the opportunity of receiving the gift of God in the assembly.

Every minister could well consider whether any sermon which does not relate to or imply baptism and the Lord's Supper is really complete, and whether his people will understand the daily, weekly, and momentary use of the sacrament without his help.

A knottier suggestion has to do with the architectural solutions which will have to be explored if baptism is to be restored to the place in worship to which theology and piety commend it. No easy solution is apparent. The font should be as prominent (this does not mean as sizable) as the altar and the pulpit. Some churches have begun to place fonts at their proper place, slightly below ground near the entrance. The font is certainly a better greeting than the sign "Gentlemen," or "Buy Tickets Here," which frequently greets the worshiper. In this location the realities of entrance into the church and of access to the Lord's Supper via baptism are more apparent.

One disadvantage of such a location in our era of the fixed pew is that people cannot then see the baptisms performed. And baptisms must be seen if they are to occasion reflection on the part of the gathered assembly in whose faith they are enacted. In a pewless church the ideal would be to have the congregation move and gather around the font. We shall be grateful to the architects who can bring some solutions to the question of location for baptisms, so that more of the cleansing, initiatory, death-and-resurrection symbolism can be made apparent.

One suggestion that could issue in immediate action would be to abolish all payments to the baptizer. Any Christian (women are Christians too!) can baptize in an emergency; but in normal circumstances a called minister baptizes. Often, as a vestige of an earlier society, he is then "tipped" for the service. Picture people receiving the Lord's Supper, then taking out an envelope of money and handing it to the minister! It would be well if congregations would inquire what their minister receives in baptismal perquisites in a year, and then undertake to include this amount in his salary. Parents could then make "a baptismal offering" more in the character of the act. Those who "bear in their body the wounds of Christ" can understand how ideas of sacrifice should be associated with the vows at the time of baptism. But the sacrifice should be a fitting one directed to Christ, not a payment to the minister "for services rendered." It is often the subtle touches such as this matter of perquisites that help to make baptism a tribal rite of middle-class culture instead of a death-and-life issue.

There are other suggestions which may be considered by the people directly involved. Godparents, for example, should be chosen with great care. No one should take on too many godchildren. Praying is hard work and one is not likely to remember with proper intensity his obligations to too many children. Godparents could well be instructed by the minister when distance is not a prior problem. Godparents can be invited to the home on the annual anniversary of the baptism. Many Christian parents have begun observing baptismal anniversaries instead of birthdays. Which day is more important, the time when I physically entered this world or the day when I was born to be an heir of eternal life by the glory of the Father? A child who has to wait three or four weeks past his birthday to the day of his baptismal anniversary can enter a period of anticipation that can be transformed into Christian purpose. Cards could be exchanged at that time; numbers of the liturgical presses are now providing cards of this type. More and more parents are using baptismal announcements instead of birth announcements. New attention to the symbolism of the white baptismal robe could be salutary. It would not be a bad idea if a bored suburban housewife were to undertake the sewing of such a robe as part of her godmotherhood. Church supply houses provide candles which can be partially burned and taken home as a reminder of the baptism. None of these is a mere novelty. Each can be centrally related to the biblical idea of a simple ceremony with profound significance.

Each day might well begin, as Luther suggests, with the

trinitarian invocation and the sign of the cross on each baptized body as a token of baptism. Each Lord's Day can be a reminder of the resurrection which is refigured in baptism. Easter Vigil services, or at least stay-at-home nights on the Saturday before Easter can be the occasion for reflection on baptism. A paschal candle in the baptismal season may be used to recall the early church's "new fire" at the time of Easter and baptism.

Today we hear much of baptismal rigorism, which means that one does not lightly and indiscriminately baptize unless there be some sign of promise that the baptism will not be desecrated through neglect. This is a complicated question which the believer in God's gift in baptism cannot lightly settle. But a first step can be taken through "post-baptismal" rigorism. The Christian life can be so self-disciplined, and hence so free, that only those who know what baptism means will wish to share in it. When all Christians are thus called to be what they really are, the church will be more exactly defined and the christening ceremony as a kind of cultural tribal rite for name-giving "because it's done" will gradually disappear.

"I am baptized."

This is the reminder made with the sign of the cross each morning, or with the thought of Christ's cross in each temptation. It is the door to newness of life. The baptized person is of the family of God, by faith in Jesus Christ and the promise of the Father. He has been adopted; he is living out the residential qualifications. He is part of the covenant; he has been sealed and his life is hid with Christ in God. No matter who enacts it, Christ is the Baptizer. And the water of baptism is a gracious water of life.